DAMN CLIENTS!

in 90 Minutes

For a complete list of Management Books 2000 titles
visit our web-site on http://www.mb2000.com

Other titles in the 'in Ninety Minutes' series are:

25 Management Techniques in 90 Minutes
Active Learning in 90 Minutes
Become a Meeting Anarchist in 90 Minutes
Budgeting in 90 Minutes
Building a Website Using a CMS in 90 Minutes
Effective Media Coverage in 90 Minutes
Faster Promotion in 90 Minutes
Find That Job in 90 Minutes
Forget Debt in 90 Minutes
Funny Business in 90 Minutes
Getting More Visitors to Your Website in 90 Minutes
Networking in 90 Minutes
Payroll in 90 Minutes
Perfect CVs in 90 Minutes
Practical Negotiating in 90 Minutes
Strengths Coaching in 90 Minutes
Supply Chain in 90 Minutes
Telling People in 90 Minutes
Understand Accounts in 90 Minutes
Understanding Emotional Intelligence in 90 Minutes
Working Together in 90 Minutes

... other titles will be added

DAMN CLIENTS!

The art of building rapport and influence with your client base

Ian Welsh

2000

First published in 2007 by Management Books 2000 Ltd
Forge House, Limes Road
Kemble, Cirencester
Gloucestershire, GL7 6AD, UK
Tel: 0044 (0) 1285 771441
Fax: 0044 (0) 1285 771055
Email: info@mb2000.com
Web: www.mb2000.com

Printed and bound in Great Britain by 4edge Ltd of Hockley, Essex – www.4edge.co.uk

British Library Cataloguing in Publication Data is available

ISBN 9781852525354

Contents

Introduction

The business world would be a great place if it weren't for clients. Demanding, rude, pre occupied, inefficient, poor communicators – some of the more delicate descriptions put forward during some of my client relationship workshops.

In the next breath they can also be described as: positive, focused, inspiring, loyal and fun. Which of the two scenarios would you prefer to work within?

I predict the latter.

Clients are the key drivers in business situations. If not for them, suppliers would have no work, no income and essentially nothing to look forward too.

They create and control markets, and regardless of how we may feel about them we have to develop successful working relationships.

Once rapport is established, your influence increases and you feel more valued as a business partner.

This book offers a few tips and tactics from the sharp end of retailing on how you, as a supplier, can manage the relationship in your favour – how you can build a long and lasting partnership that profits both parties.

Get it right and your client will love you forever.

The real you

We all have a particular way of viewing the world. Some are time-bound. Being on time for meetings is vitally important; it hurts if they are late. Others are more relaxed. It's no big deal; what are a few minutes?

It is our perception of what is right or wrong, good or bad that matters to us, and we often behave as if our perception of the world is the only reality. The aim of this book is to allow people to truly connect with others and build instant rapport. In particular, if suppliers can achieve this status with their customers or clients, their ability to influence decisions in their favour is greatly increased.

To be truly effective and connect with others we have to understand that their perception of the world could be completely different to ours. In essence we can both see the same thing, disagree on its content, yet both be right.

Seeing the world as we do through a filter of familiarity, it is inevitable that we draw conclusions on what we see and feel and store them as facts or truths. Others will draw similar conclusions yet the facts and truths they store will be different.

Therefore to fully understand and connect with others we must understand ourselves. How do we perceive things? Why does it make us behave the way we do?

An understanding of ourselves also allows us to understand how others perceive us – what seems good and not so good about our projected personality.

If we can identify other personality types and similarly understand **their** take on things – what they prefer or dislike – then we become better placed to build partnerships based on mutual understanding.

To understand your personality better take a look at the following diagrams. They are divided into different colour energies red, yellow, green and blue.

Are you top or bottom, left or right? This will position you in one of the quadrants. You may merge a bit into another colour; that's ok as we have all four colour energies in our personality. Usually, though, one or two will dominate.

Clues from body language

BLUE	detached less facial expression no physical contact body more rigid business-like	**RED**
quiet reserved intermittent eye contact gentle handshake few gestures avoids touch		leans forward full eye contact aggressive impatient more gestures firm handshake
GREEN	open responsive more facial expression more physical contact relaxed	**YELLOW**

Clues from verbal style

BLUE	controlled little emotion businesslike questioning critical blunt	**RED**
'ask' style slower pace quieter speech thinks first diplomatic keeps to self		'tell' style faster pace fills silences sounds confident responds quickly spontaneous
GREEN	more emotional animated casual expressive asks personal questions	**YELLOW**

Clues from interactions

BLUE	task-focused punctual forthright independent controlling evaluates pragmatic	RED
indirect co-ordinates systematic little challenge moderate		direct outgoing less patient challenges facts focus on future
GREEN	relationships feelings easy-going flexible friendly small talk co-operative	YELLOW

Clues from management style

BLUE	RED
asks detailed questions reserved business focus little facial expression considered answers	direct inner certainty may interrupt focused questions 'tell' style
slow to approach slower speech may be hesitant pauses before replying 'ask' style	sociable, enthusiastic outgoing faster pace smile more more gestures flippant
GREEN	YELLOW

From these diagrams you will be able to place yourself in a particular colour quadrant. As indicated earlier, quite often there may be a hint of a second colour as well.

The dominating colours provide a key to how your personality will be perceived by others. Here is a guide to the personality traits of each colour:

Red
Confident
Determined
Loves challenges
Focused
Good influencer
Decisive
Forthright
Inner certainty

Blue
Knowledgeable
Detailed
Precise
Time-bound
Air of competence
Asks probing questions
Thorough follow up
Self contained

Green
Natural listener
Good relationship builder
Sincere and warm
Persistent
Considered
Fair
Caring
Patient

Yellow
Sociable
Dynamic
Enthusiastic
Persuasive
Friendly
Adaptable
Imaginative
Quick to build relationships

Can you see yourself appearing? Essentially, the words described above are you on a good day.

However, others may see things differently. Not everyone sees your natural gifts in the same way, and the words they may use could be more like this:

Red
Impatient
Controlling
Aggressive
Poor listener
Can be seen as arrogant
Pushing too hard
Doesn't wait for feedback
Doesn't care about me

Blue
Stuffy
Indecisive
Suspicious
Cold
Reserved
Distant
Questions seen as insensitive
Focus on inconsequential details

Green
Slow to adapt
Slow decision maker
Takes rejection personally
Stubborn
Indecisive
Bland
Slow-paced
Negative

Yellow
Frantic
Excitable
Disorganised
Dizzy
Indiscreet
Lack focus
Hasty
Too casual

This difference of interpretation is fine. It does not diminish in any way the natural talents identified in the earlier assessment; it simply means that in certain situations you may need to modify your behaviour to fully connect with someone whose colour energy makeup is different.

You now have a matrix guide to how personalities may be perceived. As long as you understand that others may view your strengths in a different way and you can tailor your projected style accordingly you are at the start-point of a winning situation.

For example, Karen has strong blue energy. She is asked by her manager to prepare a report on a certain issue and present her findings the following week. Having predominantly blue energy Karen seeks out the detail, the facts and figures, and the relevant research. It's what comes naturally.

The following week she brings her findings back to her manager.

'Really interesting project', says Karen. 'I've prepared a small report (of 50 pages). If we could start at page one...'

Her boss looks aghast. He has a dominance of red energy. He wants it brief, and he is too impatient to wade through the detail. 'I'm not going through that lot; where's the one pager?' he blurts.

Here we have a perfect example of people misreading the expectations of others.

What Karen needed to do was recognise that she would be presenting to a person with strong red energy (motto – be bright, be brief, be gone). She would still have prepared the detail, as that is what gives her confidence. But she would also précis the document down to one or two pages, as that is what the red energy of the manager prefers.

The detail Karen has researched means that whichever way the conversation goes she is prepared and therefore feels confident, but she would not expect her manager to go through every inch of detail with her. He will lose interest and get restless at the time being taken; red energy has a faster, more dynamic style.

Having strong red energy, he will ask two or three tough questions to interrogate the information and ensure it is robust. As Karen has prepared fully, she can answer them quickly and with assurance. Red energy dislikes dithering and waffle; it will assume you are not confident, and subsequently will not trust your conclusions. Karen's quick and efficient response sounds good to the red energy of the manager.

With the benefit of this revised approach, they are both happy with the outcome.

It is easy to mismatch our actions with the needs of others, as we tend naturally to favour our own perspective; this is what comes most easily to us. When dealing with clients we need to identify **their** personality and play to that. If we get it right we immediately become one of them and will be accepted more readily.

Rapport is established and our influence over the outcome strengthened.

The next chapter assesses more directly how to read your client and what to do to switch to their wavelength.

Understand yourself, who you think you are. Where your strengths and natural gifts can work for you and where others may perceive you differently. From this start point you can now build a picture of the world around you and where you may need to be more flexible in your approach.

Understanding others

Psychologists state that 85% of our difficulties come from interpersonal relationships.

You need to understand that people will have different preferences, expectations, desires, motivations and needs from your own, and that if you can adapt and see things from the other person's perspective you will become more effective in your dealings with people both at work and at home.

The key is to recognise personality type and to spot others' behaviour preferences. This can be done through a variety of means - observing body language, verbal style, interaction with others, and management style.

The four diagrams shown in the previous chapter can be used to identify another person's preferred colour energy as well as your own. This will then help determine how you need to adapt your communication style to meet the needs of others.

In the space below, write down the names of 5 people you know in business who are important to your success in your job. They may be colleagues or clients.

1..

2..

3..

4..

5..

Then using the four personality type diagrams on pages 10-11 above, assess in which quadrant they most typically sit.

Simply follow the following process:

1. Do they reside in the top or bottom of the grid?

2. Then, do they reside left or right?

3. Identify the dominant colour. As indicated in the previous chapter, there may be a mixture of colours; usually, however, there is one colour which is naturally more dominant.

4. Check the personality attributes applying to the dominant colour

This quick reference guide can be extremely helpful when trying to find the best way of approaching and communicating with a client. When you have identified their colour see if it resonates with the following descriptions.

BLUE		RED	
Good day	**Bad day**	**Good day**	**Bad day**
questioning	suspicious	demanding	intolerant
cautious	over complex	driver	driving
precise	reserved	determined	aggressive
deliberate	stuffy	strong willed	overbearing
formal	cold	competitive	controlling
analytical	distant	purposeful	impatient
GREEN		**YELLOW**	
Good day	**Bad day**	**Good day**	**Bad day**
encouraging	stubborn	sociable	excitable
amiable	reliant	persuasive	frantic
caring	plodding	demonstrative	indiscreet
sharing	bland	dynamic	hasty
patient	docile	enthusiastic	flamboyant
relaxed	indecisive	expressive	flippant

The four diagrams provide a quick way of assessing what kind of person you are dealing with, their likes and dislikes, preferred management style and motivations.

The next chapter describes how you can put this all together and build rapport and influence.

If you believe your preferred way of working is the only way and force it on others you only have a 25% chance of connecting and building rapport, i.e. you will connect with your own colour type only. Be aware others see the world differently and be prepared to change and step into their world for enhanced results.

Play the away game

OK, we now understand ourselves better. We have the tools to assess how others operate and view the world. How can we then change our behaviour to suit the situation and get better results?

I will say this many times throughout the book: when you establish good rapport with someone, you have a much better chance of developing influence in your favour.

There are many instances in business where deals are struck or commitment honoured simply because people like each other.

What you have to do is play the away game, and become one of them (mirror their colour personality) to gain trust. However, quite often you have very little time to make this good impression.

It is absolutely true — first impressions count.

Research shows that when someone is being interviewed for a job, the client makes up their mind on whether that person is suitable within the first 3 minutes. The remaining 37 minutes of the interview are spent looking for evidence to support the decision.

The following table is a guide on how, having established what type of person you are dealing with, you can approach them for best results and do it quickly.

You will notice that in each scenario you should behave differently. This is not betraying your personal values in life, as you will be stating the same information each time. All you are doing is presenting it in a different way, in a way that your client will understand, appreciate and like.

Adapting to others

Red – Focus on facts not feelings
Approaching: Be direct and assured, don't waffle or hesitate **Questioning:** Watch for impatience, follow his or her pace **Presenting:** Be well organised and factual **Handling objections:** Meet resistance with reflective questions **Gaining commitment:** State alternatives clearly **Follow up:** State options with probability of success

Blue – Be prepared
Approaching: Slow down, not too direct, be more formal **Questioning:** Take notes, be methodical and structured **Presenting:** Support statements with proof, demonstrate knowledge **Handling objections:** Ask searching questions to highlight concerns **Gaining commitment:** State logical alternatives **Follow up:** Don't miss details, facts, figures or prices

Green – Slow down, be more open
Approaching: Talk more slowly, be more open **Questioning:** Show a personal interest **Presenting:** Get feedback, quote benefits **Handling objections:** Don't push, check carefully to reveal concerns **Gaining commitment:** Show people benefits, ask for commitment in a gentle friendly way **Follow up:** Focus on benefits to others, confirm details in writing

Yellow — Be interested in them
Approaching: Be sociable, focus on them **Questioning:** Not too many details **Presenting:** Focus on the future benefits, tell stories **Handling objections:** Ask questions to allow them to express themselves **Gaining commitment:** Offer incentives and special deals **Follow up:** Be clear and direct, focus on the future

I'm sure that as your read through the chart above you will notice certain traits of clients or colleagues you know. Try the approaches shown on an internal colleague first, in meetings or informal situations, to get the hang of adapting your style. Once you have perfected the ability to play the away game, then move onto client situations.

By adapting your approach you will now broaden you area of influence to all personality types. You will find in particular that your 'difficult' person is much more manageable.

Good service

Consider this. When was the last time you personally experienced good service? Have a think and jot down the words in the space below that sum up what was good about the service.

....

....

....

....

....

In all probability the words you wrote down will be similar to the words below:

Reassuring
On time
Organised
Helpful
Well mannered
Polite
Informative
Good communication
The extra mile
On my side

These are taken from many of my client relationship workshops. Can you see the theme?

It's all personal, about feelings. The list does not contain any mention of hardware, kit or capital expenditure.

I remember being in a restaurant with my family – a birthday celebration of some kind, I seem to remember.

The service was terrible. You had to shout to get attention; the meals were late and each time you had to ask if they were ready before the dishes were delivered to the table. If you dared to enquire what was going on, why the service was tardy, the response from the staff was sullen and to be frank, aggressive.

This was not my party, so I kept quiet, typically British (don't cause a scene!). Then, as usual, that irritating guy from the restaurant comes along and asks, 'everything to your satisfaction?' I looked at our host. 'Well,' he said, 'the food wasn't very good.' I could have yelled. The food was fine; it was the way the staff made us feel as though we had crawled out from under the carpet that ruined the night

Service is about people and the way they interact. When was the last time you left a restaurant with family and friends having had a great time with excellent service, and said 'Wow, they must have fantastic ovens in that place.' No, if the food was well cooked it was the people who cooked it who deserve the praise, and if the service was good, that is what you will remember most. It was about enjoyable personal interaction.

Most companies are stacked full of expensive machinery of one sort or another and yes, much of it is very useful. Most though is very similar to the machinery found in competitors' business premises.

The key differentiator, however – the thing clients notice most – is the ability of your staff to provide the human touch.

We all like to be treated well - with courtesy and manners. With things on time and well prepared.

If **we** like it that way, then it stands to reason so will our clients. Make that your company aim from those at the coalface – the salespeople or account handlers, right down to the receptionist and secretaries. They all represent your company and brand image.

Your competitor can cut prices but when you sell personal service he is up against it.

Genuine rapport and good feeling between suppliers and clients is about people and how they get on. Spend as much time as you can guiding your colleagues to become 'people people' not machines.

The basics

a b c ...

Most companies provide descriptions of the service they aim to provide; it is surprising how often the actual service provided, let alone the description, fails to match the basic needs and expectations of the client.

The basics are vitally important. They are the criteria on which you can be judged against any other competitor.

In my last few years in retail I was besieged by companies majoring on added value – what they had that no one else could muster. Occasionally, I was tempted and gave them a go. Almost without exception, they fell down on the basics and were desperately disappointing. There is nothing worse than having your hopes raised and then dashed by a succession of fundamental, irritating and avoidable errors.

Each company had spent so much time trying to better their competition that they had forgotten what was needed to carry out the job.

Research has shown that it is five times more expensive to find a new client than to keep an existing one.

In the current financial climate, the life-blood of business is repeat work. Yes, it is a very challenging task to gain new business, that next big opportunity. But it is also vitally important to keep what you already have.

To do this, and keep your existing client-base you must adhere to the basics.

Think about a situation of your own.

You book a holiday abroad.

A clever travel agent or a well-presented internet site tempts you to part with your money.

What you then want is that:

- Your tickets turn up on time.
- The travel agent provides some helpful hints on how to make your holiday great.
- They provide a checklist so you don't forget anything.
- The airport check-in staff are quick and efficient.
- The plane is on time the service is great.
- Your luggage turns up.
- The bus at the other end is prompt, clean and comfortable.
- The room is ready.
- and so it goes on...

Everything goes without a hitch.

Now describe how you feel?

Just great, relaxed, happy and willing to use the same travel company again and no doubt ready to recommend them to others – and all because they got the basics right.

Make this part of your company culture.

Churchill summed it up: 'I'm easily satisfied with the very best.' Your clients will react in the same way.

Write down what are the basics of the service you provide to clients, and then challenge yourself objectively or with the help of a facilitator to see if you really fulfil all the points.

Try to be specific and avoid ambiguous or woolly expressions like 'good communication' – what does that **mean**?

Strive to explain exactly what you need to do to make your communication robust and accurate – where it's working and where it needs improvement, and how would anyone know.

If it's not immediately apparent or easy to explain, then you probably can do better. Only when you have covered all the points on your list, objectively and thoroughly can you make the claim of doing the basics right.

6 months later, go through the same process again.

The full needs of a job are fluid. Do not be tied by a formal description. Look at the function from your client's perspective, and make that your job.

Be a double bagger

Quite often when shopping at the supermarket the load you gather in the trolley seems daunting. You reach the checkout and ask for assistance in packing.

A young store assistant appears. In his head is a brief from the management: engage with the customer and make them feel comfortable.

For some reason, he decides the best way to achieve this while packing your shopping, is to have a rather loud chat with his mate who is manning the till three lanes down. 'Great night on Tuesday, I got so drunk, what a laugh...'

This somewhat individual banter is not quite what I expected as 'engaging the customer'.

While they continue reminiscing, a singular point is missed. The goods being loaded into the carrier bag are heavy – bleach bottles, washing powder, cans, cartons... and as the bag is triumphantly lifted toward the trolley ('there you are, sir'), it splits with the weight. The goods tumble carelessly across the checkout area.

This store assistant is a single bagger.

Had the focus been on the client he would have acknowledged the heavy items and a second bag would have slipped inside the first to ensure the weight was not a problem. This forward thinking approach, foreseeing the client's needs would have made the assistant a creature loved by the client – a double bagger.

Double baggers are first to offer help; they enjoy being part of a team. They want things to go well and are prepared to sacrifice their own agenda to meet that goal. They are constantly looking ahead to foresee and predict issues, choosing prevention rather than cure.

Having explained this at one of my workshops, it was great to hear the following week from one of the delegates, Sonya, who reported, 'That double bagger stuff really works'.

Sonya was an 'inplant'. She worked for a supplier but was based inside the client company. She had regular meetings with one of the client team who was always in a fluster, always too busy.

Knowing this, Sonya prepared the room for her client beforehand.

She had the client's cup of tea ready, black no sugar; the agenda was there; the work to be discussed was on the table in order; nothing was overlooked.

The client came in wittering away as usual about the latest trauma, and eventually turned to Sonya and said, 'OK, better get going; need a cup of tea first, though.'

It was there waiting, of course, as was everything else.

The client sat down with a grin, ‘I’m impressed’, she said, and eased herself into the meeting without fuss or stress. Sonya had removed that for her.

Double baggers are a rare breed, but without doubt when you meet them you will notice and appreciate their efforts.

I wished as a client many times there were more of them around.

Be proactive with your thoughts. Single bagging is easy and obvious. Double baggers can make a real difference. Look for opportunities both large and small where you can offer help and relieve the burden.

Perception is reality

To connect effectively with others we need first to understand how we perceive the world and then how others see it.

Our perceptions are coloured by what we know and what we believe; unfortunately, as we have seen, someone else (our client perhaps) may see things in a completely different way.

You have a product to sell, a service to offer. You believe it is a great product or service, better than anything on the market. The problem is, your client base doesn't seem to have got the message; they for some absurd reason believe that your competitor has a better product.

'This is madness, how can they believe this?' rants your MD. 'Our product is far superior to our competition; you only have to look at the facts. Go back to the client and explain the facts once more. They will soon see sense and give us the business.'

In their book, *Marketing Warfare,* Al Ries and Jack Trout explain quite clearly that the better product fallacy – 'truth will out, if you have the facts on your side' – is a dangerous belief. Unfortunately, the truth is what sits inside someone's head. You may disagree, but it is what you have to deal with. How do you get them to change their views and believe that your products or services are better?

Simply believing something is good is not enough. You have to convince others to share the same belief. The best way to start this process is to build rapport, gain their trust. By understanding their personality, what they like and want, you can then play the away game and provide the detail or facts in a way that they can accept with ease.

In most cases with mid to high priced sales, the client doesn't just buy the product; they buy the trust of the salesman. The two become inextricably linked. Quite often, when a sale is made, the salesman has to stay close to the client for some months afterwards, as he or she has become part of the deal. The deal was closed because the two participating sides liked each other and built a partnership of trust and understanding.

When that important job arrives, when the client reaches out for the phone, who will they ring? It must be you. Because you have instilled the perception in their minds that you are the best and only option. Make that your goal.

Presenting yourself

Getting work from a new client is extremely difficult. Statistics say you have to speak to them at least 7 times before you are likely to get anywhere. Quite often getting to speak once is an achievement.

When you do get the opportunity to pitch, don't waste it.

The following happened to me a few years ago. I visited a supposedly talented design company in London with a view to offering them a specific project.

I couldn't find the place, tucked away at the bottom of a narrow alleyway. No-one had sent a map or offered directions. In my haste I had forgotten to ask.

A walled glass courtyard greeted me. No company sign. I tugged on the nearest door. It was locked. A person mouthed at me from inside the glass partition, pointing, 'that way (dimwit), reception is that way'.

I found the door pressed the buzzer and announced myself. 'Hi, come in,' said the receptionist. The buzzer went I pulled on the door, I should have been pushing, I had to buzz again. A simple Push or Pull sign would have helped; after all they were a communications company.

By the time I got into reception, I felt a bit stupid. I had got hopelessly lost and then couldn't find or even get past the door.

I have a trick when visiting companies for the first time; I turn up early, 30-60 minutes early. In this case, I was an hour ahead of schedule. Why? To see how they perform under pressure; are they prepared and organised?

In this case they were not. 'Sorry Richard's not here,' breezed the receptionist. 'He's down the pub.' My immediate thought was, 'Oh, great – boozy breath!' Remember, you are never down the pub; it sounds slovenly.

'Come into the presentation room and I'll try and reach him,' the receptionist said.

The presentation room was awful, covered with the debris of 4 or 5 people's lunch. Always leave a room as you would like to find it. You never know who is coming in next.

The receptionist duly cleared the place up. About 45 minutes later Richard appeared, 'You're early', he said.

'Yep, I usually am'.

'Never mind, lets get going,' said Richard pointing the control handset at the ceiling. They had a projector mounted in the ceiling, or so it seemed. All that was visible were a couple of wires.

'Hmmm, that's interesting,' said Richard. 'Back in moment'.

Two minutes later, in trooped a guy, projector under arm, screwdriver in hand.

Balancing on a glass coffee table he grunted away for ten minutes, restoring the projector to its prized position.

Of course, computers in this situation are entirely predictable: they won't work. A succession of chaps came in, pushing and prodding buttons, cursing, until – hey presto – the projector, having had its fun, burst into life'.

Have a guess about how I felt at this moment. Jot down in the space following my first impressions

....

I think they had performed as badly as is humanly and mechanically possible.

Someone had borrowed the projector in the morning, and not bothered to replace it. Richard had not checked on a thing. He assumed everything would, as if by magic, be in order.

Never presume; never let fate lead the way.

Always check you have the room booked in advance and for an hour after, in case the client is late or stays behind longer. Take personal control of the situation. If you delegate, check that the individuals concerned are on target and understand their role. To feel secure you must take responsibility and manage delegation.

Rehearse, ensure you can present even if the projector won't work. Learn it off by heart. Know what's coming so the flow and pace is as you want it.

Brief your entire company that someone you wish to impress is coming in. A Marketing Director of mine in the past always went out into the workplace and quizzed a few terrified individuals on the spot.

Clear all confidential work out of sight.

A company I knew did work for Adult magazines. They were obsessed with ensuring no one ever saw the work while on a visit as it could offend. They always briefed the entire company to be vigilant. Another company would pull blinds, like those around hospital beds, to cordon off confidential workstations.

If you are using a projector, make sure that it is working and that you have the correct presentation loaded. If you are introducing someone – e.g. 'A big Welcome to Fred A N Other' – ensure you have spelt their name correctly. If you are adding their job title, check beforehand it is the right one; these details matter. They won't be noticed if they are right, but they will if they are wrong.

One presentation I attended said 'Welcome to Ian Welsh from Superdrug'. Unfortunately, I worked for Safeway.

Choose the correct people to attend; if they are in the room they must be there to contribute, not sit there as padding.
If you are presenting to one person, have no more than three people from your side. Two would be better; don't overwhelm the client. Don't sit them on one side of the table and you on the other. It's challenging, and looks like you have defined battle lines.

Find out about the right dress code. I prefer smart casual. Sometimes it pays to copy the client's style, so you become one of them. This is particularly appropriate if you are visiting them.

As Ernest Bevin said, 'Decide before you walk into any negotiation what to do if the other fellow says no.' Decide what degree of flexibility you have in your offer.

Make your presentation visual. Endless rows of words or figures are impossible to remember. Paint them a picture – something striking. People will find it easier to remember, and hence, of course, will find it easier to remember you.

Don't bore people. Observe and listen. If they are switching off, invite them in with questions; change their state and re-engage them.

If something goes awry – e.g. the projector jumps ahead or goes backwards by mistake – don't dwell on it or even mention it; just move on. Chance is, it won't be noticed. If you drawn attention to it, it will.

Most presentations look the same. Think in advance and suggest ideas that may be useful to the client. You must say or do something (preferably positive) that the client will see as memorable, something to associate with you only.

In the first ten minutes, encourage your client to speak about the job in hand and the issues involved. Listen hard, as they **will** say something either positive or negative that **will** affect your presentation. Use that information to mould the presentation in your favour.

Mimic body language. Smile when they smile. Use the same words and language patterns. Put them at ease and build rapport. My CEO at Safeway always referred to shoppers as clients not customers. If you used the word customer you were not on his wavelength and he switched off.

Ask sensible, relevant questions, probe for any issues they have and suggest how you can fill the gap better.

Without fail, ask for feedback and next steps. If you don't get any future actions out of the meeting, you are no further forward than when you started.

If you are taking them on a company tour check the route and individuals involved beforehand. Brief them on times and what to say. Never be surprised, never assume.

And of course, in case my mother is arriving, check the toilets. Are they clean? Is the paper stocked, and handwash and towels available? And make sure the door locks.

I did have the unfortunate experience of being compromised by the MD of a company I was visiting due to a faulty toilet lock. Embarrassing for both when we were introduced later.

'I think we've already met,' I ventured.

Prepare fully beforehand – it gives confidence – but keep it flexible enough to keep it fresh.

Be enthusiastic, not desperate, and of course, be passionate; believe in what you are saying; otherwise, why should they?

Presentations can be exhilarating. It's your chance to shine and be in the spotlight. Entertain and enthuse your audience so much that they want to bring their friends and colleagues back next time.

Use the right people

To expand a bit on the previous chapter, when presenting ensure you use the right people.

Your aim is impress, gain commitment, get work.

I have witnessed so many mistakes when work is being presented, often because the wrong people are present.

Why does it happen?

Ego, lack of confidence, misunderstandings.

Whilst at Safeway we had regular ‘production meetings’. The content of the meeting is irrelevant; suffice to say it was an important meeting, comprising probably four or five internal representatives and five or six external suppliers.

It was a technical meeting with lots of jargon. We always sent out an agenda to all participants stating clearly who should attend and what would be discussed.

Remember, it was a technical meeting.

At the beginning of each session there was the ritual exchanging of business cards.

Looking at a particular card, it would say – Fred Smith (Marketing Director) or Gill Jones (Sales Director).

The question would always follow: 'Thanks for coming. Looking at your card, can I just confirm you have the technical knowledge to contribute fully to the discussion?'

'Oh no, but it is my project, so I'll take notes and get back to you later.'

It happened what seemed a thousand times. The scenario now is that the meeting is stalled. Instead of decisions being made there and then, we have to wait while Chinese whispers are in play back at a suppliers factory.

I didn't mind the self-proclaimed project-owner being there so long as the real expert was at their side. But ego seemed to block the way. It's my project, so I'll go alone.

Previously at another company, when I was pretty junior I was asked to attend regular design presentations with the main board members. I was the secretary; I took the minutes.

The Head of Design was a master presenter; he had done all the courses and starred in them all.

One significant issue, however, was that while his presentation skills at a distance, to a hall of less knowledgeable participants, were great, he was terrible at one-to-one situations, where your opponent could see the whites of your eyes.

The board members were tough, really tough. No prisoners, you knew you stuff or on your way.

Our Head of Design had a particular trait when under pressure. He sweated profusely. It was instant.

On one occasion while getting a particularly severe grilling I watched a dew drop appear on the end of his nose. It bounced tantalisingly for a moment, like a cartoon film in slow motion, and splashed heavily on table. A moment of silence followed; you could see in the board members' eyes, this guy is not up to it.

They didn't back off. Unfortunately, he did. When I looked round, he had stepped back and hidden himself half behind the curtains, his confidence shattered.

His deputy was the opposite – poor at big set pieces, but brilliant at close quarters. He was cheeky, witty, quick on his feet and the board loved his irreverent style.

What should have happened was that the Deputy should have led the presentation, with the Head chipping in when necessary, the best of both skills. Unfortunately ego dictated otherwise, with disastrous results.

So many meetings seem populated with people who add nothing, or when they do, it's destructive. Choose the right person for the job; they may not be the most senior but if they are the best to close the deal, the best to get sign-on, use them.

I had a Trading Director who always gave me a hard time.

'You're not keeping me informed; bring the concepts up to me tomorrow, I want an update'. He snarled.

I'd go up and get a right mauling, I don't really know why. However, this chap got on really well with one of my team leaders, Julie. So I decided I wasn't the right person for the job.

'Julie', I said, 'Alan wants an update, could you take the work up.'

'Yes, no problem', she said and with a grin would add, 'shall I wear my short skirt?'

'Up to you. Might help...'

Julie would swan into his office, have a chat and be back in ten minutes.

'Everything OK?' said I. 'Absolutely fine' said Julie. 'Had a chat about his family, where he was going on holiday oh and a few minutes about the work. No problem.'

Now of course this is all politically incorrect and totally outrageous; however...

The morale of the story is simple: never mind the short skirt, put status, rank and ego to one side and choose the right person for the task in hand.

Your brand

My mother used to say, 'You can always judge a place by its toilets.' Essentially, what she meant was that there are clues about a culture, an attitude, a way of behaving, that come directly from the way you present yourself.

When a client looks around at your brand, and sees it as poorly considered, dated, dull and uninspiring – if the people are lifeless and disinterested – what will they think and feel?

I have visited in my time hundreds of companies – design consultancies, advertising agencies, marketing companies, production houses, photographers, printers – each one making a case for inclusion on our core list of suppliers.

They all prepared presentations, words, images, case histories, price structures. Some did it well; others less so.

But when I looked around at the way they presented their brand, did it match the words and images I saw and heard?

Printers talked about attention to detail, quality checking, and accuracy. Yet when I glanced over the factory it might be dirty, cluttered and clearly unloved. If they didn't love themselves and their environment why would it be any different with me?

I visited one factory producing food-quality printed board. Hearing a flutter of wings above my head, I watched a flock of pigeons settle in the rafters. The words of the printer on control, hygiene, professional approach didn't quite ring true. I left there and then.

Bird droppings on my cereal box in the morning didn't appeal.

Designers would talk about ideas, inspiration, and creativity. Yet the studio was dull, lifeless and lacking any kind of creative energy. You could see it in the faces and body language of the staff as well as the environment.

One particular studio I visited was different. You entered it through a shop selling their products. From the ceiling hung an aeroplane (the MD was a qualified pilot); on the wall was a penny farthing bike (they worked for the post office), and so on.... Everything exuded energy and passion for design.

I was impressed. It was different and I looked forward to their presentation. They were off to a good start.

If you genuinely feel you have something special in your offer, don't allow brand presentation to let you down. Get it to reflect your culture in every way. Let it ooze through every pore of your company experience. It makes the job of convincing people of who and what you are, much easier.

Every business is a brand. You have a name, services or goods and a culture. Align the words and images you use to describe yourself with the atmosphere you create. Everything and everyone then becomes a selling opportunity.

Be a listener

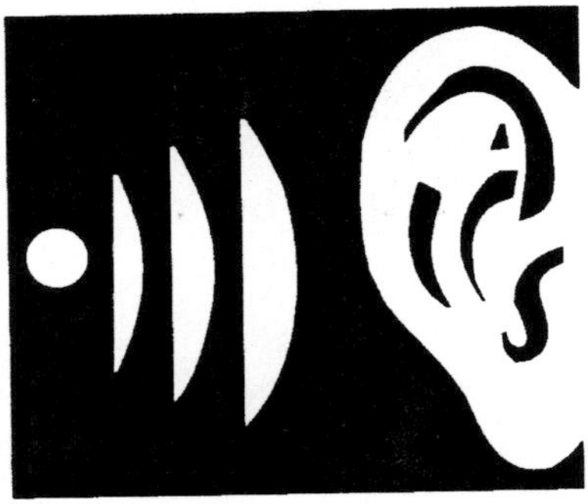

Joe had lost his filofax. Everything he held dear was in it: addresses, telephone numbers, diary, credit cards. Similar these days to electronic organisers or mobile phones.

He was completely distracted and distressed. When I pointed out that it was actually on his desk under a pile of papers, he couldn't hear me. It took three attempts to get him to switch into listening mode.

Life today can be pressurised. The task of combining personal and business needs often creates tension and conflict. In cases such as these, stress quite often takes hold of our emotions.

Suppliers can feel similarly pressured to please, make the deal or close the sale – so much so, that they become obsessed with their own situation and stop listening. They can't stop talking about themselves, their service or product.

Rapport instantly breaks down, as what they seem to be saying is, 'I'm not interested in you or your needs.'

As rapport breaks down, your ability to influence the outcome decreases.

Putting your agenda on hold and developing the skill of listening is a totally under-used business skill.

Everyone likes to be listened to. It makes us feel valued and respected.

I have sat through many supplier presentations where they were pitching for business, where all they could do was offload their opinions. 'What you need is this,' they stated.

I remember thinking: 'Do I? How do they know? These people aren't interested in my needs, the company needs, our brand. It's just a platform for their ego.'

As I said earlier, your first port of call is let the client speak; encourage them to explain their situation with careful, relevant prompts (questions) from you.

As a client, I always preferred people who had something to say rather than those who had to say something.

Listening and asking questions are critical to the understanding of needs, and fundamental to building rapport. Without it, how can you assess a client's real situation, what issues they may have, and where you could genuinely help and make a difference?

Unless you put your own agenda on hold, ask the right questions and listen to the answers you are guessing about the real opportunity. Guesswork is not a strategy.

Powerful questions

As well as developing listening skills, practice the art of asking powerful questions.

I have run many client relationship workshops over the years. Initially they were open workshops where people from diverse backgrounds and different companies attended.

As a way of breaking the ice, I always started with a discussion as follows:

'Pair off with someone you don't know and ask them three questions:

i) Their name?
ii) Their job function?
iii) The one thing they are most proud of over the past year?'

Each person then had to present back their new friend's details to the rest of the group; so it was a test of their listening skills as well.

It was a great way to get people to bond quickly, asking questions and listening to the answers – no switching off, as they had to recount their findings.

What was interesting was that the pairs of people often stayed together throughout the rest of the workshop, as they had developed a closeness, simply through showing an interest in each other.

As my business developed, I started workshops bespoke to individual companies. The sessions were now with individuals from one company or one department. They knew each other pretty well, or so they thought.

I deployed the same tactic, 'ask three questions:

> i) What's the one thing you really like about your job?
> ii) What's the one thing you are proud of over the past year?
> iii) Which person (alive or dead) inspires you, and why?'

The discussions were lively and in-depth.

What was even more interesting were the comments later.

'I never knew Fred had skied the Olympic downhill run,' or 'I was amazed to here Sue has travelled around the world and climbed Kilimanjaro,' and 'Amazing, Diane's father is the Head of the Bank of Bermuda, her surname is on the banknotes.'

Even within what seemed a close-knit team, everyone learned new things, developed a better understanding and often spoke with a renewed admiration of their colleagues.

Within a business context, dealing with clients or customers this is just the same.

When preparing for meetings we often know the script and

are very keen to offload it as a sign of our knowledge, but only give the other person little time to talk. We may therefore miss vital clues as to his or her real desires or issues.

Ask a few powerful questions to understand their motivation. What is it they want? Some are motivated by reward, some by achievement, some by acknowledgment and others by affiliation. The only way to find out is to ask and listen.

Think back to the chapter on understanding others.

Tailor the questions to their personality type. To recap:

Reds – be quick, to the point and confident.
Yellow – be lively, fun and enthusiastic.
Green – be friendly, concerned and calm.
Blue – be direct, factual and well prepared.

With these tools you are more likely to understand what is really required from this person or company and then be able to tailor your responses directly to what they need.

You should also apply this to your staff and colleagues. Show an interest in them; make them feel special about their place in life. It will help give a surge of motivation to the day, as people feel recognised and appreciated.

Always start your conversation with a question. Find out regardless of it being a new client or an existing one what they want, how they feel, and how you can help. It only takes a minute yet may give you hours of profitable success in the future.

Be an observer

From the moment you meet someone either as an individual or in a group situation, observe how they behave, what mannerisms they show, what words they use.

By observing, you can tap into their thoughts and feelings and use it to your benefit.

Whenever we meet someone for the first time, we make a fairly rapid decision whether we like them or not. Often we have no real idea of why we made this decision. It just seemed right. It was our unconscious self reacting to clues from the other person that affected our decision.

Your client will be reacting to you in exactly the same way. Therefore by observing their body language, their pattern of speech, their choice of words and the values they hold, you can build rapport and influence much more quickly by reflecting these observations back

Similarly, if you are watching people during a meeting and you see them switching off, leaning back, eyes wandering – bring them into the situation. Ask them a question; get them to change state.

When confronted by a group situation, look for the natural leader, the decision-maker. Look to build rapport with that leader. Mimic their body language, and follow their use of words, as they will probably have most influence over the outcome when you leave the room.

Watch for those that are quiet and reserved. Invite them to give their opinions as you are sure they are important. Listen sympathetically to their response.

This offer of inclusion helps build rapport and friendship – you are showing an interest, making them feel important.

If someone gives a response combined with a certain body movement or pitch of voice, you can deduce how they are feeling. It may be enjoyment, interest, or annoyance.

Remember the state they displayed. When you see it again you will understand what mood they are in.

Remember items of interest, such as their favourite pastime, football team, hobby, or family details. You can recount these at a later stage to break the ice or include them in conversation. It helps build a bond.

Observation like listening gives a huge amount of detail about the person you are dealing with. It stops individuals being strangers as you are constantly searching for clues about their real state of mind.

Never assume

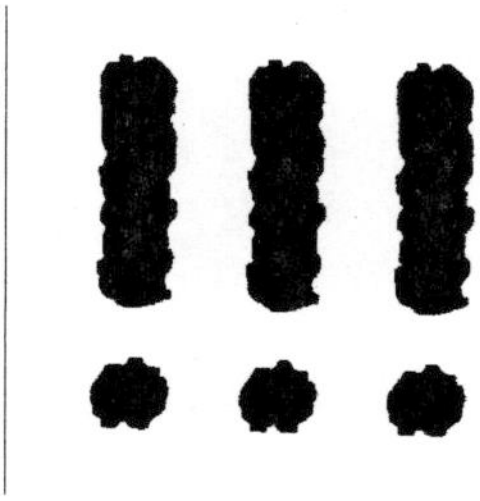

‘I assumed you were going to do it.’ How many times have you heard that statement as a precursor to an inquest?

Never assume your message has been understood; always check, summarise and ask.

I had a meeting one afternoon with a supplier Account Handler called Angela.

About two hours before the start of the meeting, I picked up my phone to listen to my voice mail.

‘Hi, it’s Angela. I need to ...**+o¬`~~*** ~##...’ Nothing but static.

She was on her mobile phone and the message disintegrated.

I rang back; the phone was switched off so I was none the wiser. In fact, she wanted to postpone the meeting, but I never knew. She simply didn’t appear.

These days, with fewer admin support staff and a reliance on technology (the curse of the voicemail), it is easy to believe you have communicated, when often the reality is far from it.

Mobiles break up. Emails disappear into the ether. Ansaphones get full or messages get erased without permission.

Years ago while, at Tesco, we were trained under pain of death to answer someone else's phone. In those days, callers always had the luxury of speaking to a human being. In these heady days of electronic devices that is not always the case.

'To err is human, but to really foul things up you need a computer.'

Always explore all opportunities to communicate.

Following the confirmation of a meeting by phone, send a letter to ensure you both jotted down the same time.

Don't just rely on one means of communication; try a backup, maybe phone and email, verbal and by post.

Following a discussion, pause and ask 'OK, let's see if I got this right, what you want is...' Check that they agree.

To confirm you all understand the same message often takes no more than 30 seconds. It is time well spent.

Whatever means are at your disposal, check your message has got through and on the same wavelength. An extra minute of two at the front end confirming detail can save days at the back end unravelling miscommunication.

Focus on them

'These guys are good. You ought to pay them a visit,' said my new Marketing Director.

I was always on the lookout for new talent, so I rang them up and arranged a visit.

I went with a young executive and met two of the supplier team. One was the MD, the other the possible account manager.

As the meeting progressed, my mind was constantly distracted by the account manager, a pretty blonde lady – not because of her looks but because for much of the meeting she spent looking out of the window or at her fingernails.

Not only did it seem bad mannered it clearly gave a message of disinterest.

Maybe the young lady had problems elsewhere, family issues far more important than meeting me. I don't know, but unfortunately this was their chance to impress.

Everyone in the room must be on top form. If you have other distractions, send someone else.

That initial one hour you spend together will either build your future partnership on solid foundations or on sand. In fact, the first ten minutes will probably clinch or ruin the deal.

Never lose concentration. You may miss that vital bit of communication, the one opportunity to ask a telling question or suggest a solution. Train yourself to keep your focus at all times. It may be tiring, but if it nails a result ...

Whether you like it or not, clients are usually selfish people. They have the upper hand in most deals, and quite often a large pool of resources to choose from. If you make them believe you are dedicated to their cause and a trusted ally they will look on you favourably.

If you just say, 'Sorry, can't do that now, we have other clients to worry about' - your days are numbered.

When that difficult brief is given, just say, 'I really think that's a bit tight. To get the quality you want we will need a bit more time. I'll definitely have it delivered by...'.

By finishing on a positive you have a better chance of influencing the outcome than just saying 'can't'.

If you can't do it, they will find someone who can.

All you need to do is repay their time and interest with a bit of interest from yourself.

Know where the line is

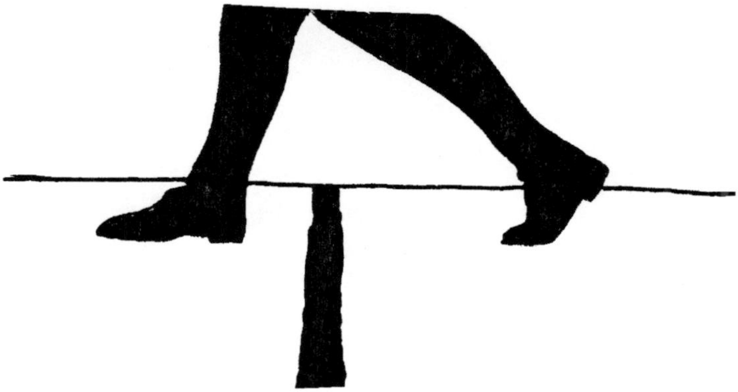

One of my team, Barbara, was a very pretty, vivacious young lady, both intelligent and capable. She got on particularly well with the account handler, Steve, from one of our core production houses. He was similarly young and handsome; they flirted regularly but with no detrimental effect on their work.

One day, Steve arrived in the office to deliver some proofs.

As he walked past Barbara, seated at her desk, he gently scratched the top of her head with his fingernails.

'Hi, Barbara everything ok?'

Barbara exploded and I mean exploded. 'Don't touch my f****** hair, don't ever touch my f****** hair....' The tirade lasted a full 20 seconds at top volume and silenced a 300-strong marketing department.

Before I could intervene Barbara had fled the office. Maybe she was having a bad hair day or even a good hair day and didn't want it messed up. Or maybe simply didn't like being touched.

Whichever it was, and despite the inquest I never really found out, Steve had crossed the line.

However small and insignificant this may have seemed, their relationship was never the same again.

Being friendly with clients, enjoying their company is great. Just be careful that the friendship does not affect the job in hand.

Never believe 'Barbara won't mind as she is a friend...'

Barbara could very well mind, and the closeness you had could easily, in her eyes, become counterproductive.

As they say, in a social environment, the supplier must never get more drunk than the client. Always be in control of yourself and aware of your actions.

Understand who you are dealing with, and never lose sight of their values or preferences.

Being close to a client can allow you to drop your defences and speak and behave out of turn. Guard yourself against these moments, as no client will ever accept friendship as an excuse for poor results or poor behaviour.

Passion

As partnerships form and rapport is established, the danger is that you become familiar with your client's needs and it becomes just another job.

Wrong, it is the next big opportunity.

I briefed a design consultancy on a brand new range of ready meals. This range was new to the market. To us, the client, it was a really exciting venture.

At the conclusion of the brief, I asked how the design guys felt. Was everything clear?

'Well,' said the Account Director, 'I wouldn't have minded some wine labels; ready meals are a bit dull'.

I re-briefed a new company the following day. We needed an enthusiastic company, someone whose start point was positive.

There is an opportunity in every situation, but unfortunately some people get stuck in their comfort zones and can't see a way out.

As they say, 'choose your rut carefully; you may be in it a long time.' Well, better not to get in the rut in the first place.

Your thinking and responses must always seem fresh, enthusiastic and vibrant.

When you are passionate about something, it comes straight from the heart; people can see, hear and feel it instantly. We appear alive and energised. People see someone who can achieve, and who wants to achieve.

Even if your audience disagree with what you say, they will love your fire and thank you for your honesty.

Some time back, a design group was asked to come up with some ideas on a re-launch of Toilet Cleaner. Now you can't get a brief much duller than toilet cleaner. Undaunted, they came up with 'Toilet Duck'. A fantastic, quirky, memorable shape and name. It stormed the market.

Passion and enthusiasm are contagious. They give momentum to any occasion. Being in a positive state helps you unlock your mind. Solutions will come much more easily.

Bring calm

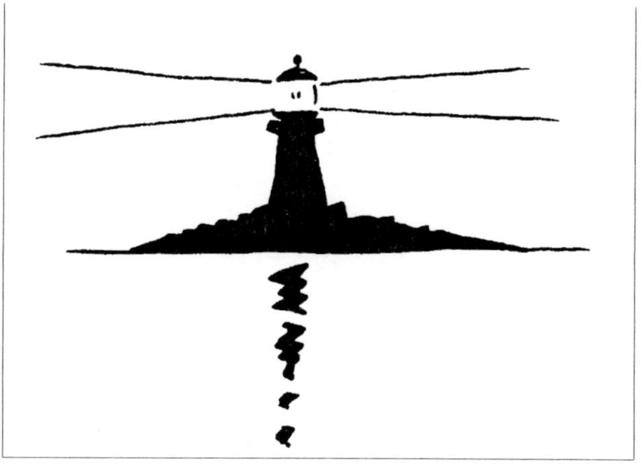

The Managing Director decreed the project would launch in-store on October 14th. I had to lead the design team who, against stifling timescales and odds, would deliver the goods.

Not only were we as a team under extreme pressure; it also came at a time when my wife and I were expecting our second child. I felt shattered.

With two weeks to go before the October launch date, I led a countrywide roadshow telling regional managers of the impending launch.

‘Great. Just what we need. About time – can’t wait’.

Their enthusiasm was ecstatic.

I sat at the back of the room having a serious panic attack. They love it. The MD wants it. And here we are with two weeks to go to launch in-store and not one of 365 packs has been printed let alone packed and delivered to store.

It can't be done, I thought. I'm going to let everyone down.

I rang my consultant print technologist who was assisting on the project, a lovely guy called Dave Sadofsky.

'Dave, I'm more than a bit concerned about the launch. How do we look?' I asked.

'No problem,' came back Dave. 'I've spoken to the printers. They are all lined up, print space booked, material ordered, and first print run due tomorrow. I'll attend to check its all OK. I reckon we'll be done and dusted in 10 days.'

I have never felt so relieved.

Dave had rung around on my behalf knowing the issues (a true Double bagger!).

He gave me everything I needed to hear, and lowered my blood pressure instantly. He was a star and safe for repeat work from me for years to come.

When problems seemed to converge from every conceivable direction and seeing the light ahead was almost impossible – suppliers (supporters) like Dave were invaluable.

The client environment can be extremely stressful, the buck stops with them. Understand their pressure points, moments of difficulty and use your vision, knowledge and expertise to offer solutions. They may not take them up but at least you have shown your concern and interest. It will be appreciated.

Politics

Quite often, as you become familiar with a client, or perhaps you become an 'inplant', working within the clients offices, you become privy to the office gossip and chatter.

It's good you are accepted, trusted and part of the family.

Beware.

You can get sucked into office politics which ultimately could cause your downfall.

I had a couple of instances in the past where this became seriously counterproductive.
One person, an external supplier working for six months in our office on a special project, became so embedded in office politics over a certain issue, she became a ringleader.

During this time, she was actively heard by many people criticising our company, the company paying for her services. She had to be removed and replaced.

It's tough enough keeping a lid on your own team at times without external staff adding fuel to situations.

You must stay impartial. 'I couldn't really comment,' or 'It's not for me to say,' or 'I don't really want to get involved, you know the situation much better than I do.'

Another supplier came into a meeting making highly personal comments about another member of our staff who he had just left in a previous meeting.

'That guy is a right jerk. I honestly don't know how he got employed, he's useless....'

Well, he was possibly right, but unfortunately in the new meeting, unbeknown to the supplier, was the jerk's best friend, who was not amused to hear this kind of derogatory remarks from an outsider.

As far as he was concerned the supplier was not there to bite the hand that fed him.

A fierce rebuke followed.

A previous chapter talks about the fine line you have to run as a supplier and friend. It's good to get into a situation of trust where clients share feelings and thoughts with you. It's actually quite a privilege to be able to help with suggestions and ideas on a broader front. Just keep it professional.

If you digress into office politics, chances are someone will hear and draw the wrong conclusions. Better to not give them the chance.

The relay race

You are sitting in front of the television. It's the Olympic Games. Onto the track stride the 4 x 100 metres relay teams.

The gun goes off, the race starts.

Our runner on the first leg is a bit sluggish.

He had a late night, a row with his partner; the press were a bit hard on him in the papers. Subsequently he doesn't put in 100%.

At the handover point, he is two metres down on the rest of the field. As he passes the baton over he shouts to the next guy, 'It's OK, you catch up.'

Well, the next guy is a bit miffed. 'What a cheek, me catch up because you didn't do your job!' He is demotivated; negative thoughts appear and he too doesn't run to his potential.

This is endemic, and goes all the way around to the last changeover. The team is now six metres down.

As the baton is passed over to the last leg runner the incoming runner says to him, 'Listen, we all agreed we wanted to win this race, win the gold – so just get down there, catch every one and everything is cool'.

Well, the last leg runner tries hard, really hard but he can't do it, he can't make up the lost time. They miss the gold; in fact they are out of the medals.

The first three runners stand around the final runner and moan, 'That was your fault, you should have tried harder, you let us down.'

How many times when doing a job or running a project do things slip. Timings get missed. Everything seems to be concertinaed towards the end of a job, and by some miracle of logic it's now the fault of the guy at the end. They have to make up for the inefficiency of others.

Clients will not tolerate excuses. They chose you because you convinced them you were the best.

It is the responsibility of everyone to do their bit, on time and in good shape. If you can't deliver your part of the bargain, then don't bother. You don't like it when others let you down; therefore don't take that approach yourself.

In successive Golf Ryder Cup tournaments between the USA and Europe the game came down to the last putt on the last green on the last day.

Most notably when Bernhard Langer of Germany had to make a final putt to win or lose the match – he missed, and the USA won. He is remembered around the world for missing that putt.

All his other successes on tour pale into insignificance because he missed that putt.

Was it his fault that the European team lost? Of course not.

What about all the other putts his team mates missed during the preceding three days? Somehow their putts at the time didn't seem as important. If one more European had sunk a winning putt during their matches, Langer would not have been in that massively pressured situation and Europe would have won.

True teams stand together; they have a mutual bond and understanding. They respect each other needs.

When things go well, true teams stand up and take the applause together; that's easy. When things don't go so well, they once again all stand up together and accept the responsibility – jointly – not apportion blame or point a finger; that's the hard bit.

Your clients aren't interested in finger pointing.

They took you on to do a good job, to manage things on their behalf.

That didn't mean just the salesperson or the team leader, who they meet and talk to regularly. It meant everyone in the chain.

Challenge yourself to make the team work and think as one and realise how important every small detail is to success. Think of those crucial missed putts along the way and how it ends with a big problem at the end.

Teamwork and the reliance on others are crucial to any environment. We must understand; we cannot do it on our own.

Take a moment.

Consider the job you do. Consider the company you work for, and the clients you have. When producing anything within this situation, can you do it entirely on your own?

Very unlikely, if not impossible!

We all call on others to help and assist. We rely on their expertise, and their knowledge. We trust them to deliver as others trust us.

This being the case, you must spend time ensuring that the team's effort to create, produce and deliver your product or service is as slick and efficient as possible. Any one weak link can destroy the entire effort.

Bring the team together regularly. Explain the job. Ensure that everyone knows their role, and never let a meeting finish without measurable tasks being allocated and agreed by all.

The power of the team when it works is fantastic. Yes, it can be punctuated with flashes of individual brilliance that inspire us all. The team however carries the day.

If you get everyone on board the ride is exhilarating.

It is often said, 'If we took away the last minute, nothing would get done.' Don't rely on the last minute. 60 seconds isn't much time in any language. Bernhard Langer didn't appreciate the last minute; he needed others before him (the team) to reduce the pressure.

Inspire

'Every great and commanding movement in the annals of the world is the triumph of enthusiasm. Nothing great was ever achieved without it.' *Ralph Waldo Emerson*

I mentioned in an earlier chapter how I asked people as part of the warm-up in my workshops to nominate someone who inspired them and why.

When the answers came, the warmth and contentment that radiated from each individual was wonderful to behold.

There was something there that was deeply personal. It moved and changed them.

I personally am a fan of Churchill. Very few people who have ever graced this planet could have managed what he achieved in 1940.

He lifted the spirit of a seemingly doomed nation single handed, through little more than the power of the radio, to a performance level no-one could have expected.

I once sat in front of a new Marketing Director. He spent 25 minutes telling me about himself.

Eventually he said, 'Ian, what do you want from me?'

I said 'Peter, I want you to inspire me.'

I have never seen such a look of bewilderment.

'Oh, well, er... I see, er... I'll see what I, er... can do...' he stammered.

Not a great marker for the future.

During my time in retail, I have sat in on hundreds of pitches and presentations.

How many can I vividly remember, that really made their mark? One. Why do I remember this one in particular? Because it inspired me. They stepped outside of the ordinary, the predictable, the comfort zone.

It was a presentation to British Airways.

I was Design Manager for a large design consultancy in London. The client party came in, five of them. They had already seen four other agencies; we were the last on their list.

For some reason our designers had bought yellow layout pads to do their initial scribbles and doodles. We usually used white.

In those days what you did for a presentation was choose the best ideas and put together a 'professional presentation' on screen or flip charts or propped up on highly expensive bits of polyboard card, coupled with an insightful and intellectual commentary from one of our directors.

Our Creative Director was, for once, hesitant.

'All the ideas are so good I can't choose between them. Why don't we use them all – overwhelm them with our creativity'.

He then ripped out the sketches and stuck them all around the walls of the room, a vast array of ideas on yellow and white paper.

When the British Airways contingent sat down, our Managing Director said, 'Don't get too comfy we're not presenting anything. Our ideas are all around you. Perhaps you can get up again and take a look see if anything inspires you'.

This they did, muttering away to each other for ten minutes.

They sat down once more and the head women said four important words, 'The job is yours.'

In all, it took about 11 minutes.

You **have** to stand out from the rest.

The trouble with inspirational new ideas or presentation styles is that they are different. We haven't seen them before, so they can frighten us.

We tend to work with what we already know and understand, because it's safe. It's familiar.

If you always choose to do the obvious don't complain when a prospective client comes back and says, 'It was a close choice. You all had good points, but...' that dreaded word 'but', the signal of failure.

Would it not be better that they come back and say, 'We had a great response but you guys stood out above everyone else.'

To achieve that, you must have a spark of inspiration that they remember above everyone else. Don't be satisfied until you are sure you have that point of difference.

A chap I knew well started his own company. He said to me, 'When I'm set up, can I come see you and present our business – see if you would like to use us?'

I said, 'Jim, I'm always happy to talk, but don't come along if you are just one of the pack. I have plenty of companies knocking on the door who are all identical. I'm not going to change my core list of suppliers for one that is exactly the same as the rest. It's too painful a move for no reward. What have you got that will lift my spirits and help improve my lot?'

He never came back. He didn't feel he could offer a point of difference. But he took my comments on board and applied them to another area of the business where he could inspire others. He found new clients and built a very healthy business; last year he sold it for a hefty profit.

Don't be content with the obvious; it is already out of date.

Stay ahead

A Managing Director I worked for in the past once said when I was moaning about someone who was irritating me:

'Don't get too worked up. We all need difficult people; they keep us on our toes'.

He was absolutely right. If everyone we worked with agreed with us, and made no challenges, we would wither and die.

The awkward ones who say, 'That's no good, I can do it better, do it my way,' help us gather the momentum to move on and improve. You just don't need too many of them at once.

I was once constantly plagued by another department who kept criticising the work and practices of my team. They basically were launching a takeover bid for the department.

I had a few choices.

One was to go to my boss and solicit support. Tricky, as she was just as worried about her own position, and wasn't going to rock any boats. 'On your own, Ian, I'm afraid,' she said in so many words.

Another option was to keep my head down and hope it would blow over. Not a chance. These buggers were determined and had high level ears to whisper into.

The third option was to stay ahead. If I could ensure that I was driving the change, on my own terms, making sure that whatever my protagonists proposed, I had already done it or was already examining it, I would have a better case.

I held them at bay for the next six years. It was tough, irritating and at times tiring.

But when an external consultancy came in to examine the company from top to bottom, my department was the only one in the entire Head Office operation (over 2000 people) that received a 100% efficiency rating.

Much as I disliked these gits (they were sly and back-handed), I realise looking back that they gave me the impetus to move on and improve. Don't wait for your ship to come in; row out and meet it.

Once on that trail, I also realised I enjoyed it. The thrill of the new gave both me and my team a massive boost of motivation and energy. We would never again drop into the rut of complacency and comfort.

Churchill summed it up: 'Ensure you lead change by the hand, before it grabs you by the throat.'

I learned from that point that I didn't need a serial protagonist to prod me in the ribs to get me going; I could (and should) do it on my own. Not only did I stay ahead. It was enjoyable and invigorating. Having others ring me up astonished, and ask how I did it, was a great boost to my standing (and ego).

The lesson is, keep ahead – don't stagnate. This is important for you as an individual, for your department and for your company as a whole. Your competitors will not slow down just because you ask them to. You must set your own pace and let others follow you.

I used to be an athlete. My club was Essex Beagles.

During that time I had the great pleasure of competing and at times training with a legend – Daley Thompson (Olympic, World, European and Commonwealth champion, twice over).

Daley was a genius in his field, but like every one he had challengers to his crown – in particular, a burly German called Jurgen Hingsen.

One training night at our run-down home at Mayesbrook Park, Barking, a guy approached Daley. 'I see Hingsen's broken your world record.' Indeed he had that very weekend.

Daley thought for a moment, then looked the guy in the eye with a wry smile. 'OK, he broke my record in some two-bit meeting with no pressure. My target is the big one, the Olympics in four months time, not last weekend. What I have to do is make sure that when I get there I am at my best. And if I'm at my best, no-one can beat me.'

Daley's attitude is a lesson for everyone. Don't be concerned about what everyone else is doing. We spend too much time looking over our shoulder thinking others are doing it better.

Row your own boat, set your own targets and get others to follow you.

Daley knew where he was going, and minor distractions along the way would not deflect him from the biggest prize in sport. He went to the Olympics in Los Angeles and had a nip and tuck tussle with Hingsen until the 7th event, the Pole Vault.

Sliding over another personal best Daley landed in the pit, somersaulted, pointed his finger at the German to make the point: follow that – what good is your world record to you now!

Hingsen was beaten. Daley took his second consecutive Olympic gold, and as a bonus regained the world record.

Set the pace yourself; make others follow you. Be a leader not a follower, and remember that history is written by winners not losers.

The 30-second commercial

This is an important meeting. You have been chasing this customer for ages. Eventually, she agrees to see you.

'Come to our building at 3pm and we can chat through what you have to offer,' she says.

Big opportunity. You prepare your presentation, rehearse your words of wisdom and off you go. In the building, the receptionist says, 'Please go to the 6th floor; Ms Smith will meet you there.'

As you stand by the lift doors waiting for the cage to arrive, a smartly dressed man arrives by your side. You enter the lift together, the doors close.

'Hi,' says the chap, turning toward you. 'I'm Richard, the Managing Director. I haven't seen you before.'

'No. I'm Ian. I'm here to see Ms Smith.'

'Great. What do you do?' asks Richard.

OK, here is the moment. You have tried for months to get to see this company, and by chance you are locked one-to-one with the top man for approximately 30 seconds. What an opportunity to sell your case and make an impression!

What is your 30-second commercial?

Well it could be: 'I work for so-and-so, and we produce great stuff at really reasonable prices. I'm sure if you gave us a shot we would do a great job and you will love us forever'.

Just about a bland as it comes.

He will have heard that tripe from a thousand other wannabees. You leave the lift and he continues upwards. By the 7th floor, he will have forgotten you completely.

As Design Controller at Tesco and Safeway, I used to receive 20 to 30 enquiries a week from people wanting to work for us, or join our core list of suppliers. About 70% of the enquiries were bland, dull and predictable. 25% were OK, reasonably well thought through and professional. Only 5% made you think, 'Hmmm... might want to see this lot.'

Now I can't describe to you what to say on your behalf.

Each and every business situation requires a different sales pitch.

But what I can say is, make it memorable, so that when the MD next meets Ms Smith, the Marketing Director, he says, 'Met so and so in the lift – can't quite remember his name, but their offer seemed really exciting. How did your meeting go?'

My experience with prospective suppliers was through telephone calls, emails, faxes and in particular a proliferation of brochures.

Being in the design industry everyone had to have a brochure.

Can you understand the exasperation, the total demotivation, every time I opened another brochure that was to all intents and purposes exactly the same as the one before.

It all blurred into one.

Do some research to find out what prospective customers want. Research your competitors to find out what sales pitch they are making, **and better it**. See who has just won a good pitch or piece of business. Ring them as a prospective client and see how they behave towards you. What are their tactics? See what you can learn and use for yourself, but make sure you improve on it, so you can make your own approach different and more memorable.

Think about how **you** react to unsolicited mail through the post. What works, what doesn't?

I once sat in on a workshop with a journalist. She was there to help us write better reports.

She said, 'Make sure you get the main message in the first third of the report, as most people won't read any further. Imagine you are working for a newspaper. You know the editor is going to come along with a new 'hot' story and cut out your second half anyway, so make sure the first bit is good'.

The 30-second commercial is the same. No long-winded essays here.

What can you do to grab the headlines in the first third of your:

- Telephone call
- Brochure
- Lift discussion
- Meeting at the theatre
- E mail
- Text message
- Advertisement
- Poster

When the curtain goes up and the spotlight shines, are you ready to perform? After thirty seconds, will they applaud or throw rotten vegetables?

Watch the science

Or more accurately, don't blind your client with science.

As an expert in your field with a highly desirable product or service to sell, you will inevitably learn all you can about the technical aspects of production or delivery.

You may even have developed the product or service yourself, and can't wait to expound in detail the fabulous offer you have.

Thing is, clients quite often are pretty ignorant about the technicalities. They know what they want but don't necessarily know how to get there.

As a young Design Manager at Tesco, I was frequently asked to attend the print runs. Basically, you stood in a print factory at the back end of a whacking great print press watching cartons or rolls of film being printed.

Now, I knew about the job in hand. I'd managed it from inception. I knew what colours were right, what quality I wanted. I wanted to be proud of the finished piece. It was part of my life.

So imagine the disappointment when the print minder hands me a piece of something I don't really recognise. Supposedly, the final printed sample. 'There you go lad, that's the best we can do.'

'Hmmm...' says wet-behind-the-ears me. 'It doesn't look like my concept, or the proof I agreed two weeks ago'.

'Oh yes, *but...*' (that damn word again) the word of failure, the word that cancels everything that has gone before. 'Yes you did very well *but* we need to do this...'

It is much better to substitute 'but' with 'and'. It stops the defensive feeling the 'but' word gives.

'You did very well *and*, if we can focus more closely on this...' Suddenly the whole tone of the conversation has changed.

Anyway, back to the printer. When I mention I'm not happy with the result what I get in response is the technical argument.

'Yes, *but* you need to understand, the way the toggle switch works in conjunction with the grommet plug means we can't align the splitt top to get a continuous squeak from the rubble-stuffed rear end.'

In other words, translated into layman talk: 'This is as far as it goes sonny; butt out'.

Not content with that put-down, he then invites another cohort from his little word of dark science to join the discussion. They now speak in a language alien to me, full of technical jargon. I stand to one side feeling like some stupid, ill educated spectator. Eventually they stop talking altogether and converse in a series of grunts, whistles and knowing looks.

Just a minute. I'm the client here. This is my job, appearing in our stores, with our logo. I think I have voice on how it should look.

Clients are usually not as well versed as you are on the technicalities. That is why they called you in to assist in the first place. The quickest way to lose rapport is point that out.

Your job is to ease them through and make them feel proud of the finished job.

They want to have success and you are the guardian angel who will make it happen. Hopefully they will learn a bit along the way as well.

You are out to make them feel good, to boost their ego. Once you start knocking them and their knowledge, they will usually react with aggression.

I actually knew a printer who, after a few moments of conversation with client, would stare hard into their face and ask, 'Do you actually know anything about print? Let me tell you...'

It didn't really bode well for future work.

I made a vow. I would never know as much as these chaps (it was their full-time job), but I would learn enough, especially a few key words. It is quite amazing when they start their little game if you throw in few bits of technical jargon of your own.

'Suggest you go back and check register or take a look at the progressives, they were fine. What's your dot gain in the mid tones? Are you holding against spec?' This was usually followed by a stunned silence as their minds clanked over the dreaded question, 'Does he know more than we thought?'

Whether you are a supplier, customer or client and you are you are not sure about something, ask. If you feel the discussion is stagnating, and perhaps becoming a source of frustration, use open questions to stimulate dialogue.

The use of:

- What?
- Where?
- Which?
- How?
- When?
- Who?

will engage individuals in a discussion that is non-threatening. It asks for their advice, and as most people feel they have an opinion will be only too willing to divulge.

Examples of good questions to ask in the situation described might be:

'The colours are not as I expected. **What** can we do to improve things?'

'**How** can we improve the register of the colours...?'

'**Which** option is best from here? **What** can you suggest...?'

Clients are not a source of amusement and ridicule. They are choosing you for your particular expertise. Repay that trust with integrity and diplomacy.

Body language

Research suggests communication is 7% words, 38% the way we say them and 55% body language.

If 93% of communication is interpretation rather than factual verbal assessment, no wonder people often miss the complete message.

It is fascinating to watch others communicate. When people are deeply in rapport they will connect with each other at a subconscious level, body language being a prime example. We all do it quite naturally.

The most common patterns are:

- legs and arm positions
- body posture
- head positions
- gestures

- voice patterns
- fiddling with pens or hair
- simultaneously tapping of fingers or feet

As we know that our chance of influencing someone will be at its greatest when they like us, we can use these patterns to our advantage.

Do not, however, make the mistake of trying to **interpret** body language; it's easy to make a mistake.

Crossed arms do not necessarily mean I'm in a defensive mood. In my case, having a bad back, I find crossing my arms particularly when standing is more comfortable, or I may just be cold.

What is more important is mirroring the other person's state.

When people like each other, they will begin the harmonised body dance of mirror imaging. When one person makes a gesture or changes body position the other will follow. In your next meeting watch people; see if they are in harmony with each other or out of rapport.

To establish rapport with your client, mimic their body language – not obvious, exact copies, but a subtle matching of state. If it goes well and mirroring is developed, change your body position and see if your client follows. If so you are being accepted and they probably like you.

You are now in a much stronger position to get your views accepted.

Putting your body in a similar position to your client will help match their state of mind. It will help you to bond and be liked. Immediately you are in a much stronger position to influence.

Honesty

'Sometimes you have to lie. You just have to; there's no other way out.'

An interesting comment from a delegate at one of my 'Client relationship' workshops.

'Well, two things,' I said. 'Don't get caught, and don't presume clients are stupid. You might get away with it once, but a second and third time will become a very obvious pattern. Rapport will vanish instantly and probably the sack will follow.'

I have seen so many people dig themselves into holes that eventually bury them. The first lie seemed plausible, but it led to another and another because they couldn't retreat. To go back on anything they had already said immediately showed them up for what they were – untrustworthy.

Plus, to be a good liar you have to have a very good memory. You have to remember not only the real situation, but also the story you told to get out of that situation, and you have to remember those two stories side by side for a very long time.

When developing my workshops, I spoke to a dozen senior managers from very big PLC companies. When I asked them to list the five most important attributes of a good supplier, each ventured honesty as one of the choices.

I had one supplier company run by two partners.

The Sales Director was our account handler. He was the guy I contacted for detail on ongoing projects. He was also a salesman who had a habit of embellishing.

'Dave, the job's late. What's the situation?' I asked.

'Oh yes, just being finished, took a while, very complex job you know. The van is waiting to bring it to you.'

It still didn't appear, so I rang the other partner, the Production Director.

'Richard, the van is late. Where is it?'

'Van!! We haven't started it yet; the machine broke down. I've got my two best guys on it now and I promise you will get it 9 am tomorrow.'

OK, I wasn't too pleased that my schedules were being messed up, but at least I knew the facts and could plan accordingly. I was less pleased at having planning time wasted through deliberate miscommunication.

One Christmas, I pulled a Christmas cracker with my family and out dropped a small red plastic rectangle, about 6 cm by 4 cm. In the middle was a white button and words above the button read 'Panic Button'. When you pressed the button up popped a spring loaded plastic flag with the words 'Merry Christmas' on it.

I took the contraption to work and stuck it on the wall by my desk, except I replaced the Merry Christmas message with the five most common excuses from some of our suppliers:

- The bike is on its way.
- It's just being finished.
- Must have got lost in the post.
- It was delivered yesterday, we have a signature (oh no we don't).
- Etc...

Every time someone rang up and said we have problem, I would press the button and see if the bad news had a familiar ring to it.

It is surprising that suppliers actually think that clients don't know what's really going on – a tad insulting at times.

It's never pleasant to have to break bad news to any client. But just consider, will that news be any easier to deliver in two days time, when everyone is hopping mad at non-delivery or misinformation? No, it won't.

Come clean, state the facts and offer a positive at the end. 'I can't do this but I can do....' If you offer positives with honesty, most people will accept it's just one of those things and move on.

Choose your attitude

There is an excellent video called 'Fish'. It's about a fish stall in Seattle, USA, and how they approach their business with energy and fun. Well worth a look.

One of the four messages they leave you with is: 'Choose your Attitude.' This struck a particular chord with me and my team.

Within any business environment (and my background is predominantly retail), there are many instances where you feel out of sorts. Things crowd in on you. No-one is working as hard as you. No-one is offering enough help – I think I'll have a good moan.

Ok, having a moan is something we all do. It helps let off steam, and can act as a bit of pressure valve. Unfortunately, it doesn't usually lead to change.

Either the person receiving the moan has their own problems to worry about, and rather than offering help counters with, 'Well, you think **you** have problems. What about me...?' or you moan to friend who is too nice to do anything but agree. You think, 'My moan must be right, my good friend agrees with me.'

Fish will tell you differently. You have a choice.

If you arrive in the morning and decide this is going to be lousy day and you're going to be really miserable, the chances are you will.

On the other hand suppose you come in and say, 'Actually it's not so bad. The sun is shining. I'm doing a job of my choice. Come 5 o'clock'ish, I'll be on way home/to the gym/to the pub. Let's make the most of it.' Then things probably won't seem so bad. The day has got off to a positive start.

We all feel stressed at times. But when you look back, in most instances you overcame the circumstances giving rise to the stress; you solved some problems and came out stronger, perhaps even feeling proud of your achievements.

People need not see every problem as a negative. As someone famously once said, every problem is an opportunity in disguise.

If you have a long 'to do' list for the day, make sure you do the most difficult job first; everything after that will be downhill run.

Clients love enthusiastic suppliers, people who seem to have positive outlook on everything, with a real can-do attitude. Everyone has the potential to be that enthusiastic supplier; you just have to embrace the correct attitude.

At Safeway we had a post boy called Isaac. He was the Fish Video in person. Isaac was an Elvis impersonator in his spare time and always had a cheerful demeanour. He could chat to anyone – me, you, the Queen – and had no side whatsoever. He always said hello, and acknowledged your presence with a permanent grin.

One morning, I was hunched in my office looking fierce, concentrating on some issue, when Isaac walked in carrying a parcel. He strode over, pointed his finger at me and sang, 'You ain't nothing but a hound dog...' Upon this rendition he then handed me the parcel and strode out again.

I couldn't help but smile.

In three seconds he lifted my spirits and set me up for the day. It made such an impression I still recount the experience regularly.

Isaac was a natural, and wherever he is now I wish him well. He taught me that day and on many other occasions that you can indeed 'choose your attitude'.

It's an easy choice. Decide to have a positive outlook and enjoy life ...or not. If things aren't going so well, be positive; decide to change and find a new challenge. Don't just sit there and accept that misery and moaning is the only way.

It worked for Isaac and his influence rubbed off on many.

Choose your attitude. Carry a positive approach at all times. Your enthusiasm will be appreciated wherever you go and open many doors to work and friendship. Most people are as happy as they choose to be.

Teamwork

As they say, your most important company asset goes up and down in the lift every day – your people.

I discussed earlier the need to ensure that everyone worked as a team. It is impossible to do anything on your own.

Within every organisation there exist politics, private agendas, ambition and selfishness. Big or small, all companies have pockets of the above to greater or lesser degrees.

There also exist charity, selflessness, respect and rapport.

The task is to get the balance right, so that those who want to achieve are fulfilled, those who want stability feel safe, those who want harmony are accommodated, and so on... For a manager or director, this is quite a task.

As a manager you also want energy, motivation and a will to achieve that takes you forward.

I once asked a senior director at Safeway about the importance of the team and team harmony.

He said, 'If you set yourself a target at the beginning of the year to achieve 10% more (however you decide to measure that 10% is up to you), and achieve it, you can be really proud of your self. But if as a manger you get 10% more from everyone in the team, then think what you have.'

The power of the team is immense – much more than any individual.

The best teams permeate all levels. They operate throughout the supplier's organisation. They deliver their goods and services in a quick and efficient manner. Everyone knows their role and respects the need of others.

A smart client will embrace its supplier's knowledge and expertise as an extension of its own. It makes the supplier part of its thinking and planning. It invites the supplier in to make a contribution. Remember, we cannot do it on our own. The client and the supplier are in many respects part of the same team.

I had a number of core suppliers, each one vetted and chosen carefully against our needs.

Having selected them, what was the point of shoving them out in cold and insisting I knew everything and would have them jump to my calling only?

I counted up the number of people within each company in my supply base. It came to over 500. That meant I now had access to 500 more brains to help take my area forward.

As a department we had four 'inplants'. These were individuals from outside companies placed inside ours. They had desks, telephones, computers, and so on. All within our building.

They were invited into all our departmental meetings. They attended our brainstorming days, our away days, our social gatherings. They were part of the team.

We met for reviews and visionary meetings to consider what the future held, and how we could all contribute to get there.

Yes, we had confidentiality agreements, but most of it was on trust.

The suppliers responded with enthusiasm and ideas.

Suddenly a whole new area of knowledge and experience opened up. They felt valued and respected, and their contribution was vital.

Even though essentially these guys were competitors, they knew there was enough work for everyone and by pooling ideas we could all benefit.

They all understood however the importance of an earlier message in this book – know where the line is. They knew that just because they were accepted into the team, this did not give them a license to become involved in politics, and they knew that just because they were closer to the client they could not rely on the notion that 'so and so won't mind, because they are a friend'. Yes we would mind. They still had a job to do and complacency would be the death knell to our relationship.

It is essential that suppliers and clients alike embrace the notion of total teamwork. There is a continuum here. The job starts somewhere and ends somewhere. Along the way we have dozens our people involved.

The best way to get from one end to the other is with

assistance of the team in total.

Take a look at your own chain of events.

Where can you improve? Who can help? What can you do to improve? Who do you need to involve and speak to achieve better results?

I always liked the saying, 'There is no 'i' in team', until the TV series The Office came along adding, 'No but there is a 'me', if you look closely.'

Never mind the joke, our individual contribution is vital. It can be the difference between success and failure. However, if you magnify the effect through everyone in the team you will realise how importance the notion of teamwork really is.

Just think, if you can get 10% more efficiency from everyone in the team, how much can be achieved and how much better life will it be.

Smile

You know my problem is, I look dour.

I think I'll have an operation to lift my features into a permanent grin – you know, like some of those gross exhibits of plastic surgery you see in the press.

A number of times people have come up to me in the past saying, 'You OK? You look angry, worried, upset...'

Actually I was fine, I just don't always show it.

I had an awakening some years back. I had to go to a psychologist and be tested; this was to see if I was good enough to be promoted.

He talked to me for 2 hours, taking copious notes. I sat three different test papers to assess this and that.

I had 360-degree feedback sheets filled in by my colleagues, peers and manager.

All done, I had to go back twice to discuss the findings and how I could improve.

What was amazing was how the little things could make such a big difference. Because people misread my facial features they thought I was unapproachable.

I came in every morning with things, ideas, issues buzzing in my head. I would head straight to my office and barely acknowledge anyone. I was intent on getting the day underway quickly and efficiently.

My colleagues were affected by this. I was intense at times fierce-looking, not interested in them.

One lady in one of my 360-degree feedback forms said, 'Actually he has a lovely smile, but seldom uses it'.

The trouble was, I thought I was smiling, but no-one saw it.

Every morning from then on I changed my routine. I would learn from Isaac the Post boy in a previous chapter. I would acknowledge all I met along the way. I would drop my bag in my office and go out and greet everyone in my team so they could see I was actually in a perfectly happy mood and my door was open for anyone.

I would smile more.

Every so often members of the team would bustle into my office, 'I just met the Chief Executive on the stairs. He asked my name, what I was working on and how much he looked forward to seeing the work in store when finished. I'm chuffed; he showed an interest in me'.

The CEO would wave and smile at people as he left the car park in his Jaguar. People remembered this as a real positive; this guy was on their side.

Conversely I also saw the effect of the Managing Director in exactly the same kind of situation.

'I just passed the MD in the corridor,' said a colleague. 'Didn't even look up. Walked straight past as if I wasn't there. What a pig.'

Years later, at the conclusion of some of my workshops, as a wind-down, I asked people to think up ideas on how they could improve their lot within the office or with their clients – how they could make more of each others company'.

They only had five minutes, but on each team sheet completed, guess what, every single sheet contained the word 'Smile'.

I ask them all how many people have children. Usually a smattering of hands (including mine) rise into the air.

'How long did it take you to teach your child to smile?'

You don't. It happens naturally.

'How did you feel when you saw your child's first smile?'

Fantastic, it is one of the high points of having children, when they beam back this lovely natural response.

So, if smiling comes that easy to us all, and it makes us feel so good when we receive it, why don't we smile more?

We actually use far fewer muscles when smiling than when wearing a frown.

When working with your client make the experience as

pleasurable as possible. Smiling at the right moment, showing the human side of your personality as well as your professionalism work wonders in tandem.

A simple smile, a wave, a moment to stop and show interest in someone, they all have a huge impact on how we feel and behave. These are great gifts we mustn't waste them.

Make smiling part of your daily routine and watch the positive effect on both your colleagues and clients.

Embrace change

In an earlier chapter I discussed different personality types. Some are energetic go-getters, ideal for sales and selling. Some are formal, time-bound and detailed, ideal at getting things done.

Some, and those with a lot of green energy, like stability. They don't like surprises and feel comfortable with what they know. They are great people people, good team players who have a calming influence.

Unfortunately they hate change.

Whether we like it or not, change is all around us. Things change these days at the most alarming speed.

Ever heard of the acronym ROCOC.

It stands for - rate of change of change.

To explain ROCOC, think of the humble typewriter. Early in the 20th century you pressed a key, up sprang a lever, which thumped against an inked ribbon, which left the mark of a letter on a piece of paper.

This basic format was still in use when I started work in the late 1970's. Yes the machine has changed shape a bit and was probably a bit smoother and reliable, but essentially it was the same. The rate of change since the early 20th century was small.

Think now of today's computer – the successor of the typewriter – and how every new model has marvellous new additions.

The rate of change these days is massive. The change curve from being a steady incline is now virtually vertical.

Every company has to change and adapt. To do that, the individuals within that company have to change as well.

For some, change is hard. They are coming out of their comfort zone, into the unknown.

This is a communication exercise. Tell them why we are doing it, the benefits to them and the company. Provide training and guidance to help manage the transition seamlessly.

Many companies force change on staff and expect them to piece together how it works in the office place. For many, that is very difficult. They are now disorientated and anxious about the future; quite often they will choose to leave, rather than face the trauma of uncertainty.

That uncertainty and a public acknowledgement of diminished performance will be noted by your client; they will sense the anxiety and act accordingly.

Establishing a culture of change is imperative to survival. Your competitors will not stand still on your behalf. Your clients expect innovation.

At Safeway, 60% of sales came from products launched within the previous two years. That shows how thirsty customers are for new things.

Change can be difficult. You take the plunge into new waters and it takes time to find your feet. You stumble along thinking, 'Why did I do this?' Persist – it is the route to success.

'Don't worry,' as my hero Churchill said. 'Success is going from failure to failure with no loss of enthusiasm.' And similarly, John F Kennedy said, 'Those who look only to the past or present are sure to miss the future.'

One of my suppliers was the biggest company of its type in the UK. Across Europe there were only one or two similar companies in Germany who could claim to match its turnover and client base.

I was amazed one day when visiting to see one of competitors having a tour of the factory.

I asked the MD, 'Mike, is that Manfred from your main rival?'

It was.

'Aren't you worried he will pick up some ideas from you, take them for himself? Don't you need to keep your place secret?'

Mike looked blank. 'Why? I'm way ahead of him in systems, technology and people. For him to catch up will cost a fortune and take two years. By then I'll have moved on again, and he'll still be way behind'.

Essentially he was saying, 'So long as a rival follows in your tracks, he can't pass you.'

Mike was a serial change addict. It was ground into his company culture. Everyone on his staff knew they would be moving on, and constantly offered ideas to push things forward themselves. They knew Mike would listen; every comment was a potential winner.

What he had achieved was not only establishing the need to innovate as part of everyone's job; but he had also developed employee empowerment, where ideas came regularly from the bottom up.

Because the staff felt they owned part of the idea already, getting them to sign on and change was all the easier. This was their baby as well and they were keen to nurture it into life.

Mike's philosophy was clear: 'When a good idea comes into your head, don't give it a seat; put it to work.'

Change is essential. Adapt or die. Communicate, educate and train those that need to join you on the journey. When you have achieved your aim and reached your destination, change again.

Seek feedback

Why are so many people scared about what others think of them, and how their personality, behaviour and performance are perceived? Or how their work is being received?

I did a workshop recently which started with exercises aimed at finding out everyone's personality style.

One lady said to me beforehand, 'But what if I don't like the results?'

Well, tough to be honest, you are what you are; this is how others perceive you. If you don't like the result, then this is the starting point for you to establish change. Without it, you will never know.

Of course, at the time I was far more diplomatic than that.

I have met many companies who, having just lost a major client account, bemoan their situation.

‘Honestly, we never saw it coming. Everything seemed OK. No-one was giving us bad comments, or telling us things were wrong. They just rang up one day and dumped us’.

Or even more sinister, the work just slowly dries up and you are left with nothing, including no explanation. When you ring up, no-one seems to want to talk to you. You have achieved hero to zero status.

Quite often what has happened has been a cumulative process.

A few things go wrong, which is no big deal. A few more happen, which becomes irritating, until eventually someone at the client’s end says, ‘This isn’t right.’

At that point, the magnifying glass comes out. Everything starts to be scrutinised in detail. Little things that in better days would go unpunished suddenly become major issues.

And all the time, no-one has said anything to you.

Believe it or not, not all clients are aggressive bulldogs spoiling for a fight. Most are just ordinary people who have happened into a situation and want as easy a result as possible. They don’t want confrontation; they want harmony.

When difficult issues come along they don’t necessarily want to make big deal out of it; they rather hope it will go away and mend itself.

So after a while, having endured more and more problems, rather than confront the issue head on, they simply move away to a new supplier and hope for better luck.

It’s the easy way out. No arguments, no haggling, no justification of right or wrong, just a new supplier who is only too willing to service the account to the hilt.

And all the time you thought you were doing fine.

I have seen this scenario many times.

To avoid little issues festering and becoming big ones, be proactive.

Always look for feedback.

Too many people are too keen on asking how **well** they did, rather than try to spot potential weaknesses. Quite often we make sure we ask the people we know will give us the right answer.

When I was being tested for a job promotion I had to hand out 360-degree feedback forms to colleagues, peers and my manager.

Basically, they had to describe me warts and all.

Did I hand those sheets to people with whom I had difficulties, people I didn't like or get on with?

No bloody chance. I sent them to people I hoped would give a good report. Everyone did the same. Therefore, was it a true reflection of how the majority of people perceived me?

In business when you seek feedback from only those you get on with and ask, 'Was it OK for you?' the chances are that they will be nice to you and give the good bits. After all, they like you; they don't want to hurt your feelings.

Make sure you include:-

- How can I do better?
- What else would have helped
- What was wrong with it

They are now much more likely to give you an honest answer.

As a client I was all powerful, with £6 million quid to spend. Companies were queuing up to do business.

Whenever a company worked with us, periodically I asked them for feedback on our performance.

Unless I knew the truth, how could we improve?

Don't be frightened of the truth, it's out there being discussed whether you like it or not. You might as well be part of that discussion rather than be excluded.

Employ the best

A Director of a major US company once said:

'We take on the very best, we give them the best facilities and training, we pay them the best salaries and then, if they can't hack it, we fire them'.

What he was saying was he was going to give everyone the best opportunity to do the job well and make him money. If, with all that behind them, they couldn't do the business then he could offer no more; they had to go. But at least they couldn't complain about lack of support.

Too many companies skimp on people and the salaries they pay. Yes, salaries are the biggest expense in any company, but would paying a few extra pounds to get a really good employee be money wasted?

Quite often there seems be a perverted sense of fun in knocking people down to the lowest level. A bit like bargain-hunting – I feel good because I got a deal.

I had a supplier in the north who was struggling. Every supplier review showed them at the bottom. They weren't performing horrendously, just not as well as they should have been.

I visited them a few times to set objectives and improve performance, and I was struck by the different faces I met each time.

There was always a reason why people had moved on – they wanted to go around the world, they had an offer they couldn't refuse, they needed to look after a sick Aunt...

On one trip, the Managing Director took me out for a meal in the evening and brought his wife along, a charming lady.

However charming, it is always risky to bring wives or girlfriends along. They are not always as circumspect as you would like.

After a few drinks, I mentioned the changing faces to his wife. 'No surprise there,' said the lady, 'he pays peanuts – always has done. Who wants to stay in a pressured environment with no reward or prospects? They stay a few months, suss they place out and rush for the door. He would rather have the money in his pocket than give to someone else.'

Good job the guy didn't hear, or the trip home would have been a bit feisty.

It made sense. He was good at covering his tracks and supplying plausible excuses but the bottom line was becoming all too evident. The people on his books weren't good enough. He was taking on the lowest quality staff, primarily to feed his own personal lifestyle.

There are two key issues here. Taking on the best costs money; keeping them costs even more. But in all probability the good'uns will keep your existing clients happy and tempt new ones in as well; the poor ones won't.

Most people know the best chance to negotiate a salary is when you are about to join. The company wants you on its books and is more likely to listen to your views.

Once in, however, you are stuck with what they give you because the only alternative is to leave. Not everyone wants that hassle on a regular basis.

So what happens? They are good – that's why you took them on – but they get suppressed on reward and get demotivated. Soon, their work suffers and a bright spark becomes an also-ran. What a waste for them and for you.

I mentioned elsewhere a friend of mine, Jim, who started his own company. He made a point of taking on the very best. In fact, the company looked totally top heavy in the beginning and you wondered how it would survive, with big salaries and little work.

He persisted and soon they became known for their outstanding quality and service. The client list grew. Few, if any, were disappointed with the results.

After five years they were bought out and Jim was repaid for all his efforts with a hefty payback.

Would they have reached that same situation and been so tempting to a large American company if Jim had taken on a succession of juniors at the lowest possible wage?

An interesting conundrum and obviously a huge initial risk. But for Jim and his colleagues in the end it proved well worth it.

Another common failing is when people hire individuals they can control – individuals who are not as good as them.

Wrong! Always take on people better than yourself; otherwise your department or company will be suppressed to your level and that may not be enough.

They don't have to be better than you at everything; but they must be stronger, more accomplished at something. If you take on, say, five new people, all better than you at something, and you are confident with your man-management skills, just think what potential you now have at your disposal.

Beside that, you can learn from them, and at the end of the day, the success you achieve together will be taken as a reflection of your own astute leadership qualities.

Take on the best – better than you. Reward their effort fairly. Never suppress talent through miserly behaviour, because their demotivation will become your burden.

Meetings

How many times has this happened to you?

You end a meeting and ask, 'Everyone OK? Everyone clear on what to do? Great, we'll meet again in two weeks.'

Two weeks later, when you reconvene and ask, 'Right, how did everyone get on?' you are then greeted by:

'I didn't realise I was supposed to do it'.

'I thought old Bill was tackling that one'.

'Didn't we agree we had another two weeks, that's what I heard?'

And on and on.

How can this happen? We all heard the same things. We all agreed we were clear on next steps; we all knew the timings.

Yet when the moment comes we all heard differently.

There are numerous books adorning many bookshops that tackle in depth the art of running meetings. I do not intend to compete with any of them.

From my experience, and no doubt the experience of all too many others as well, many meetings by and large are incredibly wasteful. As they say, 'meetings end with minutes and waste hours.'

Keep meetings brief and specific.

Ensure only those who actively need to participate are there.

Keep the numbers small. Four people is a good size. It's intimate; no-one feels threatened; everyone can hear and participate. Once above four, the meeting tends to fragment into separate factions who discuss things amongst themselves.

I have heard people moan so often about the number of meetings they **have** to attend. Interesting words those - **have to attend.**

Do you really have to attend, or is it to boost your ego that you are there? Or maybe you are frightened of missing out, perhaps handing the initiative to others?

If you sit in meetings all day, all you do is absorb information, and never have time to do anything with it. Therefore what's the point of being there?

A Marketing Director of mine once said to me, 'There is only one person in charge of your diary, and that's you. Don't waste the opportunity to organise your life.'

Decide whether you are the right person to attend.

Decide whether by attending, you will help things happen. Essentially will the boat go faster by you being there?

Prepare. Even if it is only for five to ten minutes. If you are going in cold with no agenda, find someone who can fill you in on the details so you feel confident.

The following is a perfectly true story. My manager was given a new boss. The new guy worked in a different building three miles away. My manager's phone rang; it was his new boss's secretary.

'Mike, Mr Newguy wants to see you right away. Can you get down here within the next 20 minutes?'

'Sure,' said Mike, keen to impress.

Mike walked into Mr Newguy's office, pen and pad at the ready.

'You asked to see me' said Mike.

'Did you bother to find out why I wanted to see you?' said Mr Newguy.

'No', said Mike, 'I just came straightaway.'

'Well', said Mr Newguy, 'next time make sure you do – goodbye'.

Quite what game Mr Newguy was playing we will all have an opinion on; his point however was rammed home.

Prepare and make sure you know what I expect of you, next time.

When running a meeting, there are a couple of tactics I have always found useful.

When involved in a meeting with a number of people, some of whom you may not have met before, play to the natural leader of the group. They are the ones most likely to influence decisions when you leave the room. Mimic their body language, use their vocabulary, understand their colour type from the earlier chapters:

Reds – be here, be brief be gone.
Yellow – be enthusiastic and fun.
Green – show concern, fairness and understanding.
Blues- be sure of your facts.

Set a framework for the meeting.

Invite everyone to state their personal objectives for the meeting at the start, so they feel involved and not ignored. When dealing with diversions or distractions, refer back to the personal objectives established at the beginning of the meeting, and ask how this particular topic is relevant. If it isn't, then offer to take the discussion outside or to a more appropriate forum.

Summarise periodically what you have heard. 'OK, what I believe we have just agreed is this...' or, 'Everyone all right with that?' Then move on.

Repeat the process at strategic moments to ensure the group has a common understanding. It also reminds people of past decisions and avoids going over old ground.

Network. If possible, meet or discuss the agenda with meeting attendees beforehand to gauge how they feel about certain issues. It may pre-empt discord and also give you an ally if the topic is contentious.

Meetings have a place but only to advance situations. Use them sparingly but efficiently and you will be amazed how much time you then have to actually do things.

Be organised

Be organised. Common sense really.

We all need to be organised to live our lives. How else would we catch the train to work, plan our holidays, or arrange to have friends over for dinner?

Why, then, does every major company around the world run copious workshops on:

- Time Management
- Organisation skills
- Delegation
- Personal effectiveness
- Etc...

Organisation is about prioritising what has to be done, and when it has to be done, for maximum effect.

When preparing for some of my workshops, I asked a number of leading client company managers what they expected from their suppliers. Being organised featured in every list.

There was, however, a contradiction here. When I asked a number of suppliers what personal skills they needed to improve to help them progress nearly every one included: time management, organisation skills, ability to delegate, personal effectiveness.

They didn't see being organised as an existing personal core strength. This can't be right I thought. This is your job, providing organisation for your clients.

What became clear was that front-of-shop personnel - the salespeople and account handlers – often were yellows. They were gregarious, social, enthusiastic people. They were great at sitting around a table engaging others and making life interesting. What they were poor at was making it happen; it didn't come naturally.

When looking at a team you need a mix of individuals and have to match their skills to the job in hand.

Quite often it is hard to find one person who can do the up-front selling and also make it happen effectively from there on.

One chap I knew was a fantastic salesman. As a colleague once said of him, 'Bob can open doors others can't even find.' He then added, 'Mind you, once he has opened the door get someone in quick to help him, as he'll lose the opportunity just as quick.'

Bob sold the story; but he couldn't deliver it himself. Therefore he needed others to move in and work alongside to ensure things happened.

It goes back to a previous chapter; ensure you have the right people doing the right job.

What you hear on so many occasions is the cry, 'I didn't have enough time to do it.'

Well, didn't you? There are 24 hours in a day, seven days in a week. How much more time do you want?

The crux is not that you didn't have enough time to do a particular job, more like you prioritised other things ahead of it, and quite often we prioritise the things we like doing or are easy. Essentially, we all find time to do what we really want to do.

When drawing up a 'to do' list as many of us do every day or week, put at the top of the list the job you least want to do - do it first and the whole day then seems much easier. It's like a massive weight is lifted from your shoulders.

You know there is nothing more satisfying than getting to the end of the day having completed all your tasks, with nothing hanging over for tomorrow. Try and make that your daily aim. If you can't achieve it on your own, ask for assistance or advice. Always remember, 'Asking for help is a strength, not a weakness.'

Similarly, if you say you are going to do something there are only two options:

1) Do it. Effectively and on time.
2) If for some reason you can't do it, tell someone and suggest an alternative.

Often, if you are honest about a problem and suggest options on how to redress it ('I can't do it by 11am, but it will definitely be done by...'), most people are happy to listen.

It's when you don't say a word and don't deliver that they get angry.

As I sit here now, I am waiting for a delivery of furniture from a well-known retailer.

They were due to ring between 7am and 10am to confirm delivery.

Did they do this? No.

I sit in and wait, and then I ring their constantly engaged number to find out what's going on. Eventually at 11.45am I get through. They say, 'We will deliver sometime before 5pm.'

Why did they not ring me?

Why could I not rely on their organisational abilities to make my life easier and more relaxed?

Why did they not keep their word?

Why have I spent half of the day waiting with no information, getting frustrated?

I could have used my time better, yet a supplier of mine decided to make that difficult.

Will I be in hurry to use that company again? Probably not.

Being organised is a state of mind. Use it as an opportunity to make both your day and that of your customers and colleagues more fulfilling.

Finale

A few words of wisdom from others. I don't know who coined them but I thank them; they all fit in somewhere.

'A person's character is like a fence; it cannot be strengthened by whitewash.'

'Better to keep your mouth shut and be thought a fool than open it and remove the doubt.'

'It's easy to be generous with other people's money.'

'We are all manufacturers – making good, making trouble or making excuses.'

'You wouldn't worry about what people think of you if you knew how seldom they do.'

'When people complain of boredom they usually have done nothing to deserve it.'

'I find when I sleep on a problem, all that happens is I wake up in the morning with it still there, but more crumpled.'

'Some people have a one-track mind with very little traffic on it.'

'In killing time, see to it that you do not murder a big opportunity.'

'There's always a cheap excursion ready for someone who wants to go to the dogs.'

'Deal with the faults of others as gently as you deal with your own.'

'Beware the half truth; you may have got hold of the wrong half.'

'You cannot build a reputation on things you are going to do.'

'People do not plan to be failures, they just fail to plan.'

'Never underestimate the propulsive effect of a pat on the back.'

'Vision without action is a daydream; action without vision is a nightmare.'

'Either that wallpaper goes or I do.'

'Footprints in the sands of time are not made by sitting down.'

And finally remember – nobody on their death bed ever said, 'I wish I'd spent more time in the office.'

Have fun.